ANDREW LLOYD WEBBER™

FOR CLASSICAL PLAYERS

Andrew Lloyd Webber™ is a trademark owned by Andrew Lloyd Webber.

The musical works contained in this edition may not be publicly performed in a dramatic form or context except under license from The Really Useful Group Limited, 17 Slingsby Place, London WC2E 9AB

To access companion recorded piano accompaniments online, visit:
www.halleonard.com/mylibrary

Enter Code
2697-6362-9322-2153

ISBN: 978-1-5400-2641-5

HAL•LEONARD®

Visit Hal Leonard Online at
www.halleonard.com

Contact us:
Hal Leonard
7777 West Bluemound Road
Milwaukee, WI 53213
Email: info@halleonard.com

In Europe, contact:
Hal Leonard Europe Limited
42 Wigmore Street
Marylebone, London, W1U 2RN
Email: info@halleonardeurope.comm

In Australi, contact:
Hal Leonard Australia Pty. Ltd.
4 Lentara Court
Cheltenham, Victoria, 3192 Australia
Email: info@halleonard.com.au

CONTENTS

CATS

   4   Memory[1]

EVITA

   10   Don't Cry for Me Argentina[2]

JESUS CHRIST SUPERSTAR

   17   Hosanna[1]

   20   I Don't Know How to Love Him[2]

   26   The Last Supper[2]

JOSEPH AND THE AMAZING TECHNICOLOR® DREAMCOAT

   29   Close Every Door[1]

THE PHANTOM OF THE OPERA

   34   All I Ask of You[1]

   38   Angel of Music[1]

   45   The Music of the Night[2]

SONG & DANCE

   50   Unexpected Song[1]

Pianists on the recordings: [1]Brendan Fox, [2]Richard Walters

The price of this publication includes access to companion recorded piano accompaniments online,

for download or streaming, using the unique code found on the title page.

Visit www.halleonard.com/mylibrary and enter the access code.

Memory

from *Cats*

Music by Andrew Lloyd Webber
Text by Trevor Nunn after T.S. Eliot

Molto espressivo e rubato

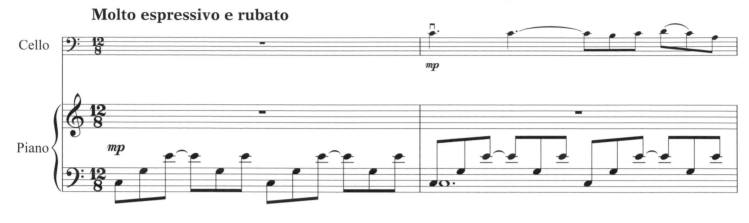

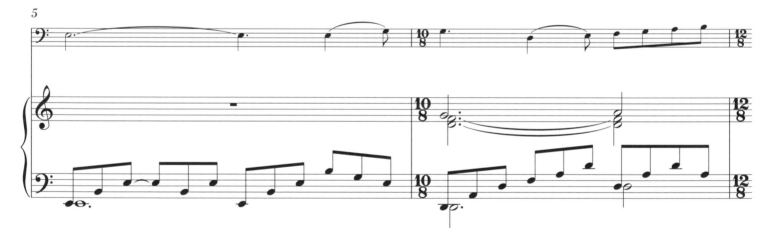

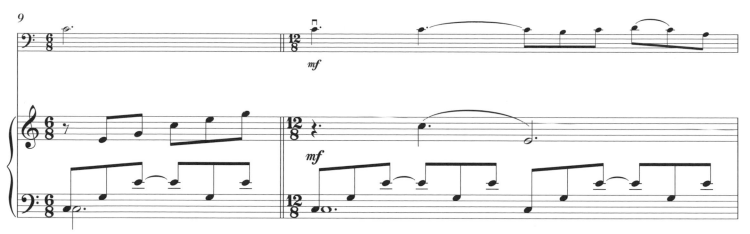

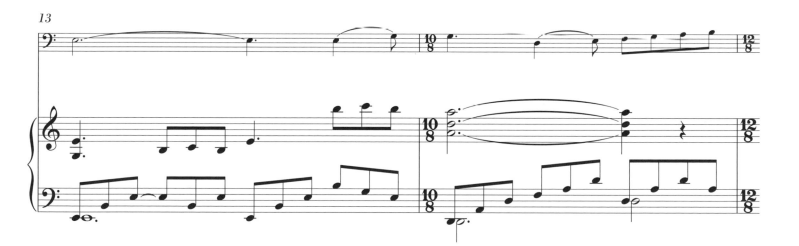

Broadly

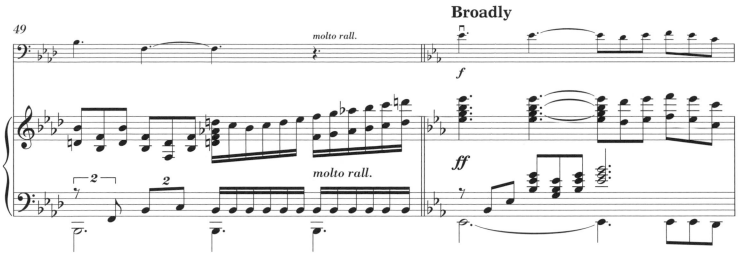

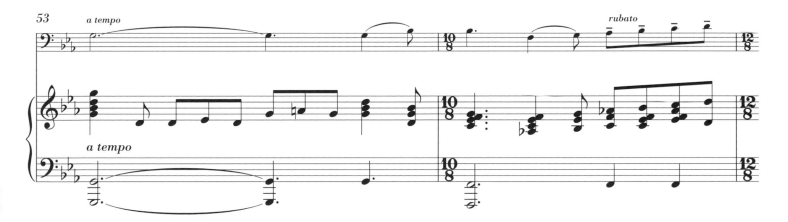

Don't Cry For Me Argentina

from *Evita*

Words by Tim Rice
Music by Andrew Lloyd Webber

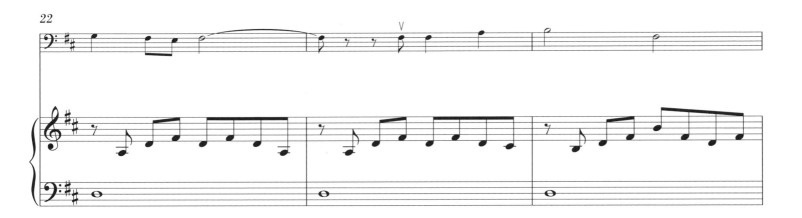

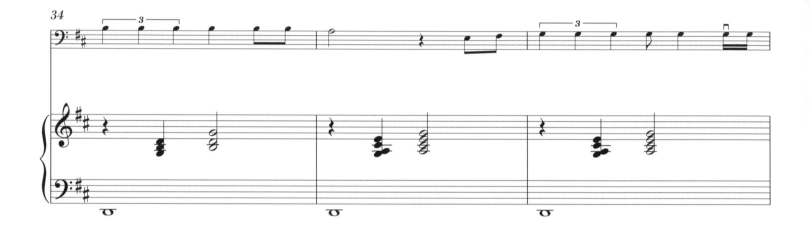

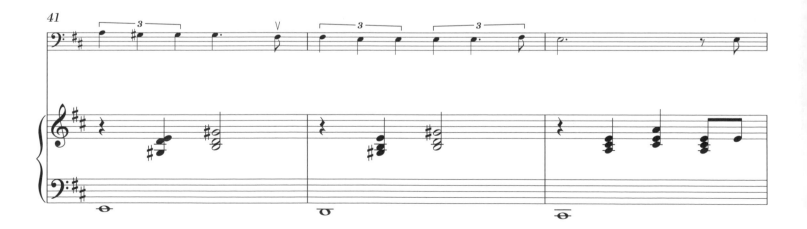

Slow Tango feel

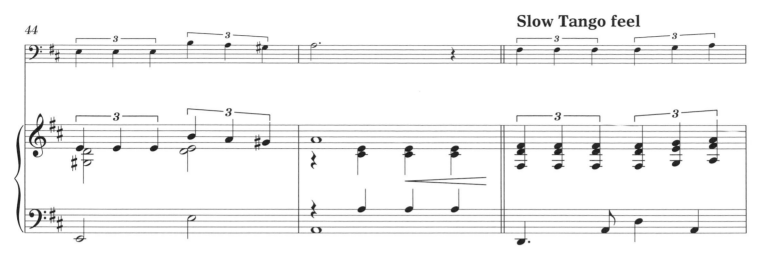

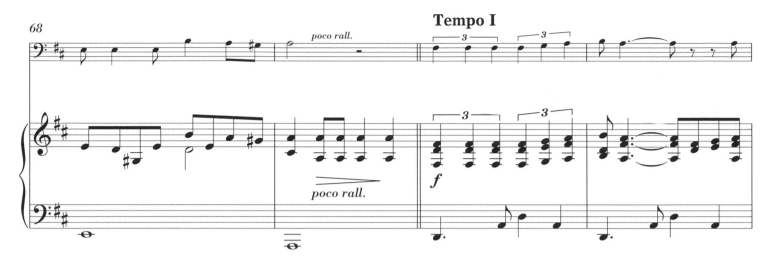

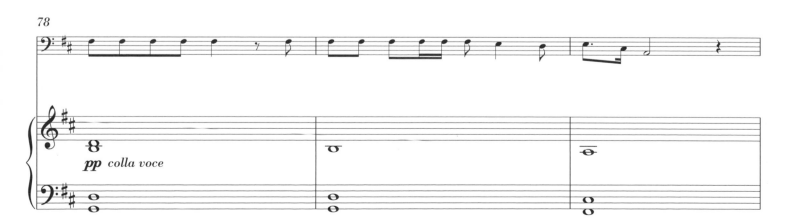

81

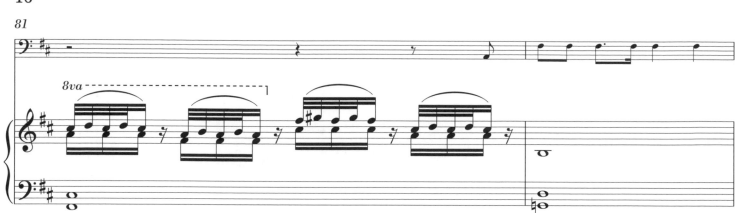

83

Grandioso

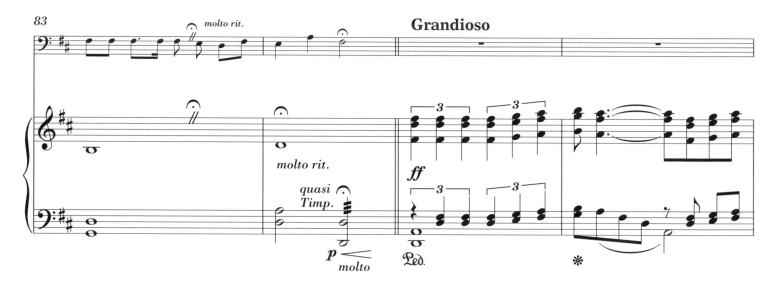

molto rit.

quasi Timp.

p *molto*

ff

Ped. *

87

8va

91

poco rit.

(8va)

poco rit.

p *f*

Ped. *

Hosanna
from *Jesus Christ Superstar*

Words by Tim Rice
Music by Andrew Lloyd Webber

I Don't Know How to Love Him

from *Jesus Christ Superstar*

Words by Tim Rice
Music by Andrew Lloyd Webber

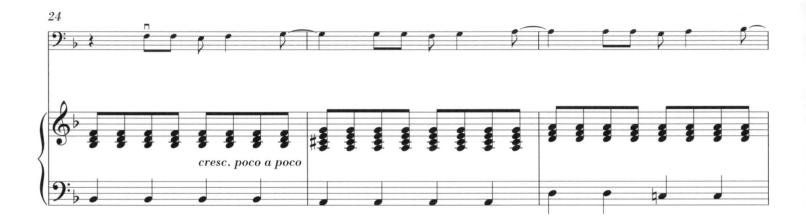

ANDREW LLOYD WEBBER™

FOR CLASSICAL PLAYERS

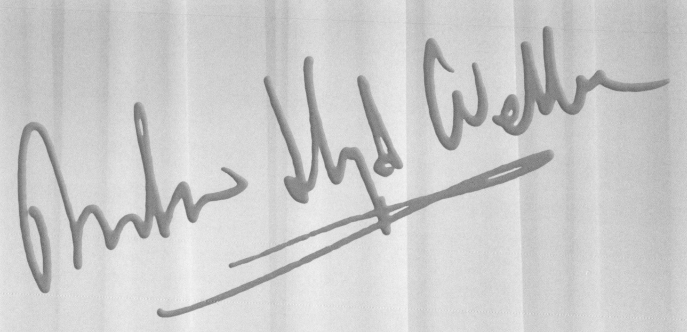

Andrew Lloyd Webber™ is a trademark owned by Andrew Lloyd Webber.

The musical works contained in this edition may not be publicly performed in a dramatic form or context except under license from The Really Useful Group Limited, 17 Slingsby Place, London WC2E 9AB

To access companion recorded piano accompaniments online, visit:
www.halleonard.com/mylibrary

Enter Code
8331-3505-0406-9364

ISBN: 978-1-5400-2641-5

Visit Hal Leonard Online at
www.halleonard.com

Contact Us:
Hal Leonard
7777 West Bluemound Road
Milwaukee, WI 53213
Email: info@halleonard.com

In Europe contact:
Hal Leonard Europe Limited
Distribution Centre, Newmarket Road
Bury St Edmunds, Suffolk, IP33 3YB
Email: info@halleonardeurope.com

In Australia contact:
Hal Leonard Australia Pty. Ltd.
4 Lentara Court
Cheltenham, Victoria, 3192 Australia
Email: info@halleonard.com.au

CONTENTS

CATS
  4   Memory[1]

EVITA
  6   Don't Cry for Me Argentina[2]

JESUS CHRIST SUPERSTAR
  10   Hosanna[1]
  8   I Don't Know How to Love Him[2]
  11   The Last Supper[2]

JOSEPH AND THE AMAZING TECHNICOLOR® DREAMCOAT
  12   Close Every Door[1]

THE PHANTOM OF THE OPERA
  14   All I Ask of You[1]
  16   Angel of Music[1]
  18   The Music of the Night[2]

SONG & DANCE
  20   Unexpected Song[1]

Pianists on the recordings: [1]Brendan Fox, [2]Richard Walters

The price of this publication includes access to companion recorded piano accompaniments online,

for download or streaming, using the unique code found on the title page.

Visit www.halleonard.com/mylibrary and enter the access code.

Memory
from *Cats*

Music by Andrew Lloyd Webber
Text by Trevor Nunn after T.S. Eliot

Molto espressivo e rubato

5

Don't Cry For Me Argentina

from *Evita*

Words by Tim Rice
Music by Andrew Lloyd Webber

Slow Tango feel

8

I Don't Know How to Love Him

from *Jesus Christ Superstar*

Words by Tim Rice
Music by Andrew Lloyd Webber

Slowly, tenderly and very expressively

30

34

38

42

50

54

58

rall.

62

10

Hosanna

from *Jesus Christ Superstar*

Words by Tim Rice
Music by Andrew Lloyd Webber

The Last Supper

from *Jesus Christ Superstar*

Words by Tim Rice
Music by Andrew Lloyd Webber

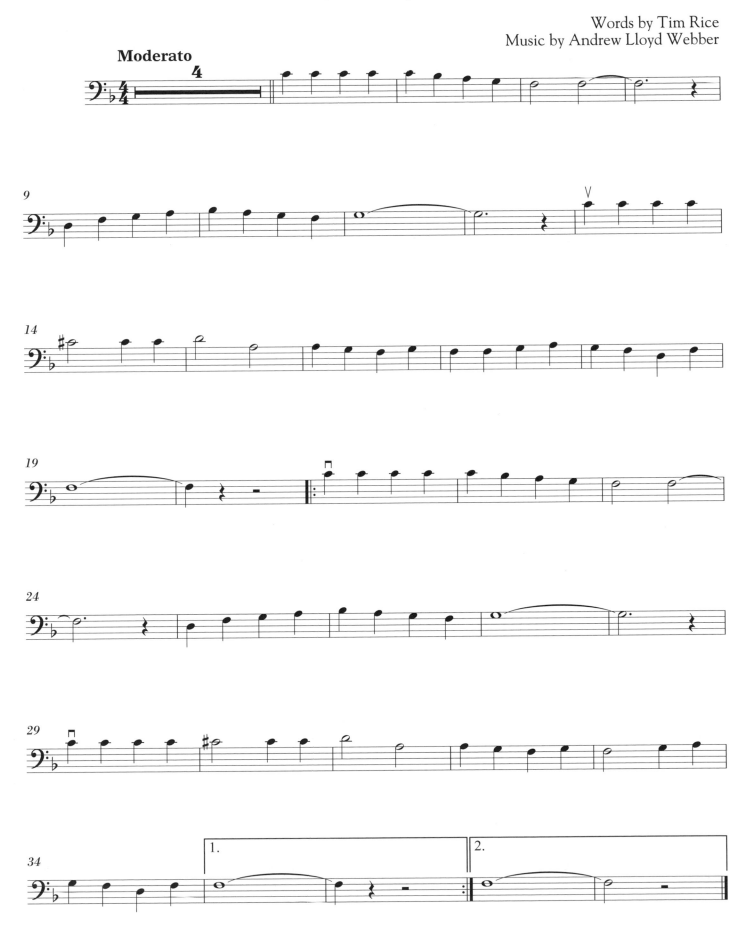

Close Every Door
from *Joseph and the Amazing Technicolor® Dreamcoat*

Music by Andrew Lloyd Webber
Lyrics by Tim Rice

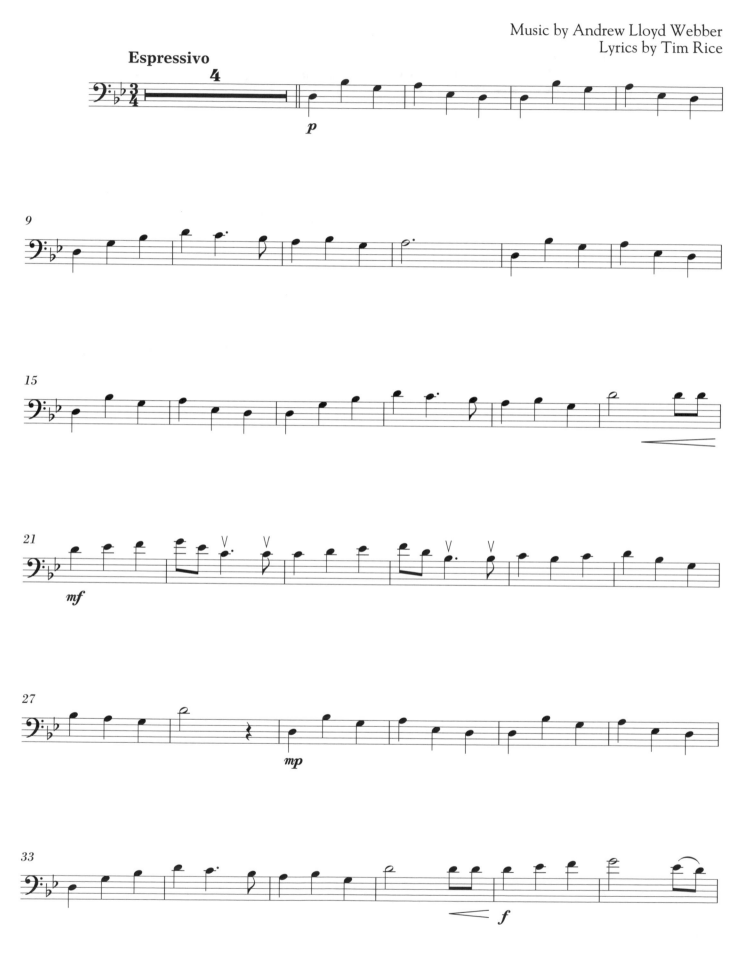

All I Ask of You

from *The Phantom of the Opera*

Music by Andrew Lloyd Webber
Lyrics by Charles Hart
Additional Lyrics by Richard Stilgoe

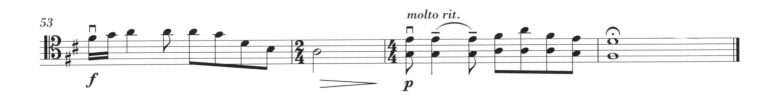

Angel of Music

from *The Phantom of the Opera*

Music by Andrew Lloyd Webber
Lyrics by Charles Hart
Additional Lyrics by Richard Stilgoe

Adagio

The Music of the Night

from *The Phantom of the Opera*

Music by Andrew Lloyd Webber
Lyrics by Charles Hart
Additional Lyrics by Richard Stilgoe

33

37

41

45

49

53

57

63

Unexpected Song
from *Song & Dance*

Music by Andrew Lloyd Webber
Lyrics by Don Black

Gently (♩ = 76)

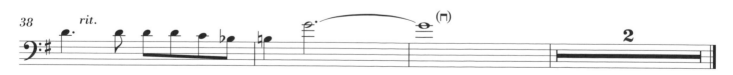

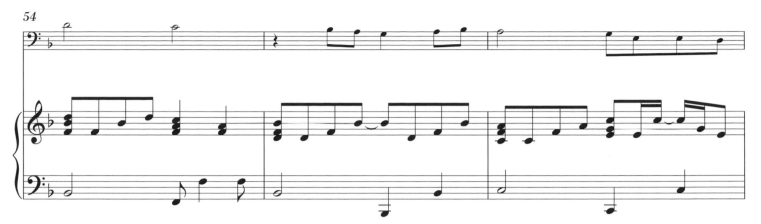

The Last Supper

from *Jesus Christ Superstar*

Words by Tim Rice
Music by Andrew Lloyd Webber

Moderato

This page has been intentionally left blank to facilitate page turns.

Close Every Door

from *Joseph and the Amazing Technicolor® Dreamcoat*

Music by Andrew Lloyd Webber
Lyrics by Tim Rice

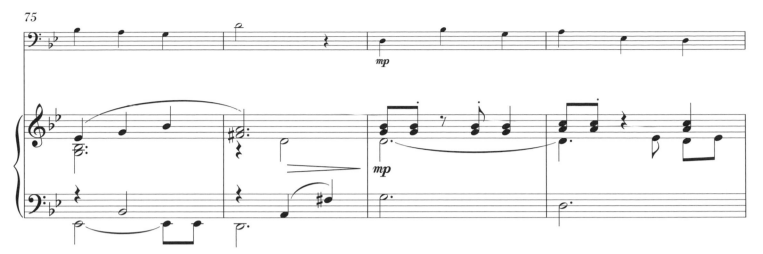

All I Ask of You
from *The Phantom of the Opera*

Music by Andrew Lloyd Webber
Lyrics by Charles Hart
Additional Lyrics by Richard Stilgoe

Poco animato

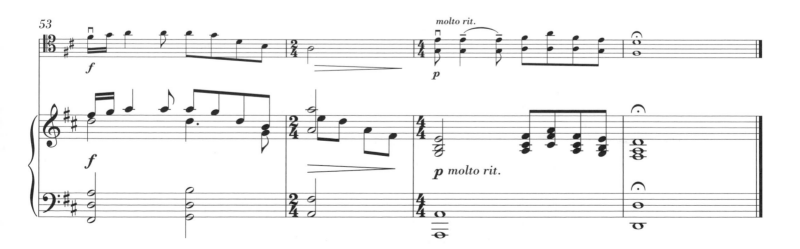

Angel of Music
from *The Phantom of the Opera*

Music by Andrew Lloyd Webber
Lyrics by Charles Hart
Additional Lyrics by Richard Stilgoe

Poco più mosso

Ancora poco più

Tempo I

poco rall.

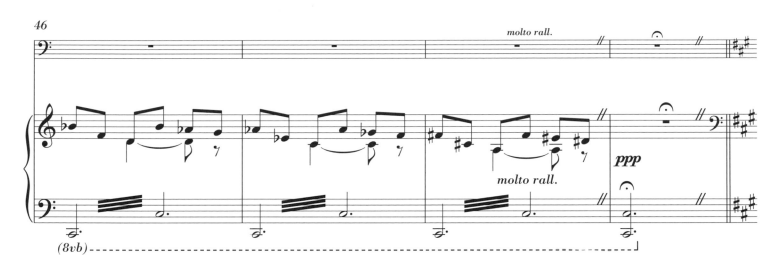

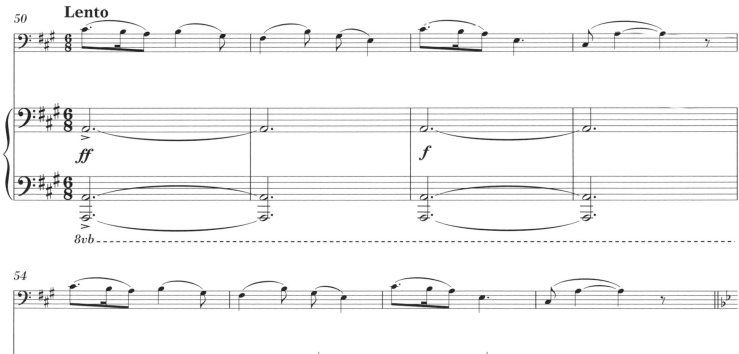

L'istesso tempo

This page has been intentionally left blank to facilitate page turns.

The Music of the Night

from *The Phantom of the Opera*

Music by Andrew Lloyd Webber
Lyrics by Charles Hart
Additional Lyrics by Richard Stilgoe

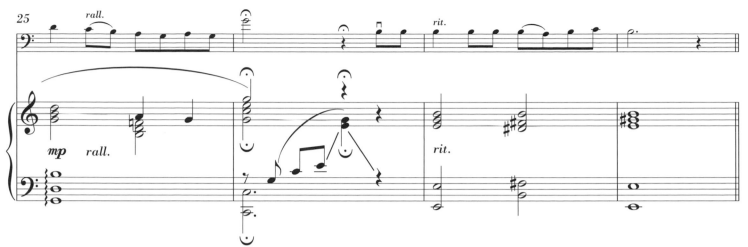

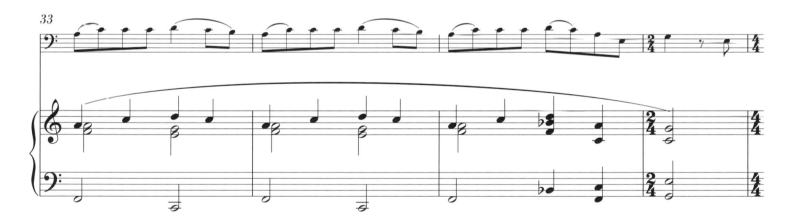

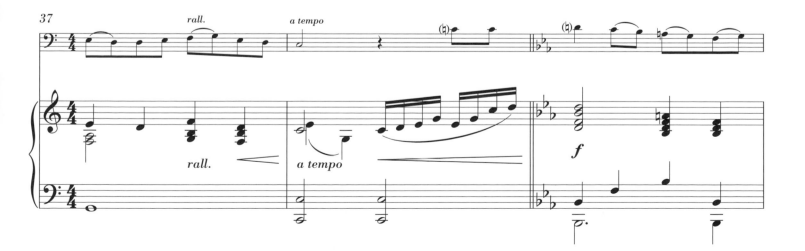

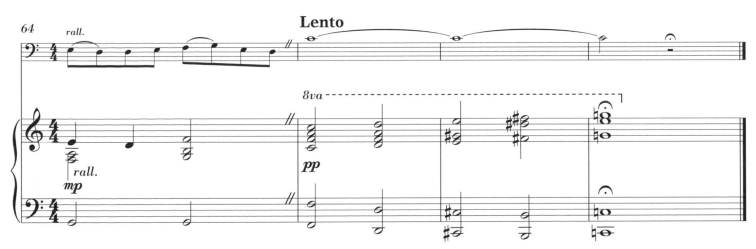

Unexpected Song
from *Song & Dance*

Music by Andrew Lloyd Webber
Lyrics by Don Black

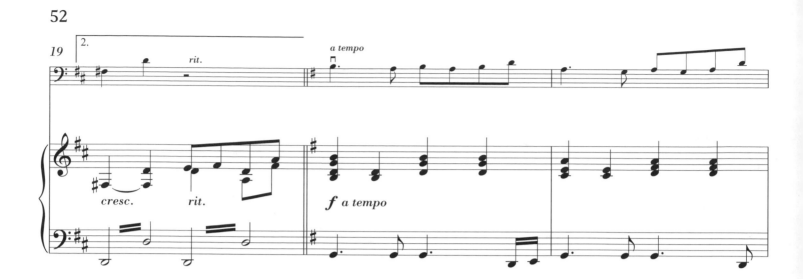